CW00548133

SPLITFISH

Kiran Millwood Hargrave

Gatehouse Press

www.gatehousepress.com

Published by
Gatehouse Press Limited
90 Earlham Road
Norwich NR2 3HA

www.gatehousepress.com

First Published in 2013 by
Gatehouse Press Limited

Text © Kiran Millwood Hargrave, 2013
Illustrations courtesy of Tom de Freston

ISBN 978-0-9566385-7-1

Cover design by Tom de Freston and Norwich Designer

Printed and bound in the UK

Contents

for Tom

Dusk House

Tea and Sea

When he entered me
I emptied myself
and dreamed of tea –
jasmine, coy
on my tongue, and
fresh mint, sweetened
in Jordan:
climbing the bright hills
with my brother;
the mother-of-pearl ring
bought at the top
by my father and
my mother; my mother
who likes her tea
English, and weak as
early morning light.
My mother, cupping
sunshine in her palms.

I found the sea shelled
in his hand at my throat
the thumb salty, bitter
in my mouth, spirited
from coasts ghosting
through: the sun
dipping as we drove to
San Francisco, wired by
discovery and the moon
beside us, sharpened
in its wane to a blade
cradled at my neck.
The submergence
into shocking cold
tides at Wells, tides
at Druidstone, tides.
This girl

she is washing away:
expelled as the piss
down her inner thighs.
I will find her
years later
crouched under an
unmentionable weight,
and changed.

Splitfish

We are lying on the ocean bed, one sea-mile down.
Our eyes ring with salt, full moons of breath sing up.

His circling boat darkens the sand to trace our outline,
until he slings hooks that catch her hands and tongue.

He draws her up into the boat's wide sides, finds the bite
of the blade in her pelvis, grunting as he guts her.

One sea-mile down, I cannot be pulled up, even as
he drops her overboard, even as the water takes our weight.

Dawn

The antiseptic stung
between her legs
when she lay, so

in the early hours she took
the path by the river,
settled to watch

a heron's stoop in the shallows,
scanning for the silver shift,
for an arrival,

both of them sorting shadows,
the moorings of her body loose,
just starting to bleed.

Flower

It blooms across her shoulder where,
in slow delay, he spilt
the vessels with deliberate teeth.

Recorded it then, and again when
it opens its reddening head and expands to
fullest effect: blood-brooch. Proof.

Branding the act in purple and green
a forest of forget-me-not
rooted in her clavicle.

In the shower she scrubs to bleed
and by a week it clings
to spider monkey black –

she dresses it lightly, in cotton.

Dusk House

The dulling chink of sun in glass,
the emptying of light from the yellow room,
in the window: the bird house, a cat
eating crumbs from its shit-mired base,
and in the sink a sluice of pink, draining –

And through the hatch to walls of red, a walkabout of fire
on dun carpet, past the walnut table and writing desk,
scratched leather surface topping deeds and currency;
a counterpane balanced like dancing, about to fade
and all the scarlet turning burns against beige –

And out into a not quite night, a seethe
of almost dark, grass thick and wet below trees
steady-dropping shadows above the wrist drip and
waiting, knees pressed against green, waiting
for that final silent rotation of stars –

Bed Rest

Rust from the door handle will tang your fingertips
for days after you enter, days spent with hands laid
decorative in your lap. The soft heat of your body will push
against the room's empty cold, turn towards the light arranged
around the window, light that does not press further
onto the wall's flattened green. Breath's a dry heave
in your chest, and under your tongue a taste you cannot name.
You number the fallen pennies of stars through the window,
guess the ones almost dying, the ones already done, or count
the beeps decoding your body to morse – learn to scent
the double tap of blood through your chest, and sense a loosening
of skin as the dust circulates, growing certain you've inhaled
a lungful of yourself.

Slice

Then came the age
of cookery programmes.
I devoured them all, watched

pears strained from their skins
in a dash of honeyed water,
the lick of the spoon and its plunge
into depths, the ripping of fat
from pummelled steak, its drip-blood
drying and the flash-fry of flesh:
its gravy'd demise.

I baked cakes of frothy meringue,
laced them with plum wine,
a communion of syrup and
sweet forgetting that parcelled
itself like burning paper
as it shrunk to a wafer
on my tongue.

But nothing topped
the drop of the lobster
into the rolling boil.

Or the opening of clams, sighing
their mealy deaths
in a steam of wine and garlic.

Cure

The one hundredth concentrate
petunia oil in water for sleep;
a dusty eighth, bought guiltily
and never smoked;
programmes for Sunday Service
(three sad months of faith);
seventeen Creme Egg wrappers;
one hypnosis CD; and a matchbox
of Norfolk sand, still holding sea.

Kowloon

Under a low moon
he hunts me down
graceless as lust
finding me just when
I had forgotten him
as I lie pressed
and twisted
in flower sheets
and I throw back
my head
and I howl –

Periphery

I think I remember you saying that the grease
at my lips was sugar-sweet,
and that you feasted, minute and fragile,
in something close to peace.

My heartbeat stuttered beneath the pins
of my ribs as your tongue flicked steadily
at my mouth, while I conjured feathers
bright, jewelling and thin.

And though while forcing in
you crushed the span of me, I think
I remember you crying too, scared
of your own darkness.

And how, at that confluence of light,
you shattered into the many shadows
I still see creeping
at the edge of my line of sight.

Playing House with Bluebeard

I build a home of skin and bone
on a cliff top by the sea,
there are no locks and so no need
for any kind of key. I weave
a welcome mat from his hair
and plant his teeth to seed,
preserve his eyes in old jam jars,
spread the rest on a red tea chest,
unpick the thousand miles of lung
so the better he can breathe.

Estuary

Kite

It is that promise of hope –

the heart's short lift
through arched, spread-eagled currents,
above England's welling pit.

Caging ribs yawn mouth-caved-wide
then bite again as each dip
skips the slow air's southerly glide.

The plunge comes always fast as shock
into some soft part,
scatters the bones' neat locks.

The sharp unpick of wind beneath wing
flights Kite home.
It trees the skyline. Its feathers sing.

My Wasps

Aged six: equipped with a jar
I soak the ground with honey
and lead their buzzing bodies

to the catacomb of glass. This new
cathedral hums psalms through my palms,
their nut-small bodies faithless, rattling.

I conch them to the cup of my ear
and they sound like darkness; purring
tigers pelted in lemon-and-black.

I place them to the centre of our rug
and in the halving light
I half-core an apple with my teeth, sit

to eye the jar,
to watch them seethe.

Days of Rest
for Laura

Sunday. And he sits alone
with *gone* burrowed into his being.
His breath mists the glass
burning at his lips. He'd like to plot

a revenge, turn her motives outwards
to pluck the seeds soft
and envenomed from her brain,
puzzle out their shooting green.

Instead he is alone in a house
where *gone* has inhabited each shadow
and shadows him
through every hour.

The telephone rings
but he is resting. Sunday.
Lets the machine coil voices
through the hallway

and parrots the intonation
of worry to parody, gone from
himself through a tumbler
slick at the ellipse.

The room tips carelessly
and the window dims, passes
into reflection. He stands,
practises the notes of his speech

and as always he is sure
to keep his words (gone for now)
sweetened. One day, he will need them.
One day, he may have to eat them.

The Blinding of G

They beat him black, blue, deaf and dumb.
His two eyes felled by the balls of two thumbs,
dropped from their sockets; two rotten plums.

Strapped him to the core
of a withering ship
slit his apple and let it drip.

Something Biblical, Ovidian, Shakespearean
in his punishment – certainly,
an ancient fear for this modern-day Tiresias.

In Mingora and London
their children sleep on,
blameless as a coin-toss.

Racing-fruit

In the garden of your third house
were rose bushes, a complete
orchestra composed in pink.

Your father crouches in slacks, careful hands
clip back the tissue paper heads of the dead,
let them drop to the cropped green.

You watch – your pocketful of berries
ready to dry and roll on the drive –
racing-fruit fit for lone afternoons.

From here he takes your fingers,
unsticks them from your palm,
fills it with his own.

Around the summer-full lawn you go,
tall-and-half-grown and together
in the blooming of your third home.

Cross

His arm unfurls
in the last of blue,
flesh laddering
against each finger of
the slow grip beneath rib,
rising at the point
where his heart
scoops his chest,
his tongue a ribbon
flag waving –
tasting surrender.

Fir Tree Copse
a eulogy

They drew in close to dusk
to Fir Tree Copse, loss
tilting them into silence.

Everything runs to grey,
smudged at the horizon line
in an ash-and-hazel tangle.

The air is moth-mired
and cool, and still
they are not speaking.

Moths come furred and fat,
wings thrumming against azure
as they melt out their existence

in the trees, blurring
their way across the bells
of petals, curled at the corners

and plaited loosely on stalks.
The day drops suddenly to night
and they are alone.

She opens the lid
and ashes tip against the wind,
are taken quickly, ounce by ounce.

His hand flutters
whitely to her waist.
They leave the path

to pass the place where
bluebells had crushed
at her back.

Worship

Beach presents the suck of sea
its congregation of one
emerging from behind the pines
shaded to menace
onto pebbles hitching
a step or two between toes.

Came here once before
in a wave of heat and pinkening men
laid out like offerings on altars
of dried samphire and striped towels,
now here again –
walked the same way to the water.

Knew the path by its lack
and the sound, of course,
moved forward until the trees lost
their thrust and I found myself on this:
the unique reliquary of stones knuckling
my soles, beneath gulls piercing the sky.

Estuary

We sought some light among the finial dark
of our parents' house – the bulbs
waxing to eclipse
and the whining of dogs outside,
seeking us: gum-limbed beasts
removed from themselves by hunger.

You turned at the stairs to our mother's study
fingered the stations of address books;
the sentinel *Mont Blanc* turned tin in the gloom;
the long-curdled tea in its Made-in-Cley mug. Here,
you found solely the glint of her catacombed body,
eyed in this dusk by that unravelling star.

Outside, the chestnut smouldered, reeking Christmas
across the lawn. From there, we had watched the birds
litter our stalled street, collected each small body
for our two cats, already unpuzzled to ribs and arthritis,
more air than bone. I eased them with a packet of aspirin
in the last of the milk, my hand on their fur, a precise knife.

We should never have left this house.
We travel by rail to see the white cliffs
chummed with suicides, the turtles brought
on unnatural currents north from an erased Asia,
and beached by bodies coupling in the scum.
We link hands to jump.

Now the dead line up to fill their cups
at the cobbled crossroads nearby,
where parents had brought their children
to look up and watch the parrots wheeling the sky –
then each barrelled a gun at each soft head,
seeking some small blessing in the cresting red.

Rain in Town

The gardens are half-toppled
by weeds and the borders

of bushes are stalked by tigers,
shrunk to tabby cats by rain,

while sodden corners of houses
wheeze damp up the fireplaces

and churn out mould, as solemn heat
gathers at the window panes.

The greying streets confess
to a kind of undoing,

their rosary lights strung across
pavements in imitation of safety

precise as compass turns around
their small circles of loamy light.

Muted coats hunch home
to jaw each day's small calamity

at waiting families. The evenings
lope across the clock

and wind up to the final quarter
as the nights turn

over to fill the absence. Dreams
tick and spiral. Rains rise up

to cover the fireplaces, but the fires:
still they burn.

Grace

In the moments of his leaving himself
    his hands shook and could not take mine.

Instead he stared
    and handed through the silence

the slightest cup of my chin
    rolled my cheeks between his fingers

like dough, and in those seconds
    he still needed me,

and it was a blessing as complete as bread.

Inside the night-time minutes
    he held me with this gaze

until the slender tap of knuckle
    at his throat wound back and down.

I touched my palms in prayer
    to stay the longer held in that stare

as the trimmed nail of his tongue
    lay still, and settled clasped into its last grasp.

Breathing Lessons

Fossil

When called she comes
from somewhere deep, speaking
behind water, each word a fossil,
perfectly cold, found.
Break them

from their bedrock
and they hold form enough
to prove the rock unravel
of their channels
carry no pulse,

and all that's left are
the fragments of nothing living;
not skin, not blood, not bone.
Still, pocket each

until they rub to dust.
Make them precious. Tell her the way
her words break, lace together, break,
is like the sea,

like salt already dissolving,
like air delicious and full
in your mouth.

Wheeling

I pearl-dive into you
on a single held breath
taut inside my ribs –
my heart cupped into its cavity –
with a world of minor insanities
curling around us,
harsh as rumour.

My hands circle deeply
in the dusk and find yours,
a rotation simple as weather.
For a while we are
a certainty that needs no name,
wheeling into each other's lives,
safe and sure as seasons.

Trinity Lawn

He rolls a grass blade between left forefinger and thumb,
the narrow sprawl of his back white on green, exhale
dicing through dark.

The sepulchral night arches around us
and the willows throw hanging shadows;
warning of sudden drops.

Breathing Lessons

The white patience of your hands, soothing
the pate of my face, its numbed curvature,
learning how not to touch me, and how
on certain nights we cannot stay in the same room –
the heavy jar of my books jamming the gap
between door and carpet

to keep you out.

And how you pressed your thumbs into the hot shells
of my ears to tune out that difficult dark, held my forehead,
hummed until I found your frequency,
and eased the unlovely pressure from my chest
with careful touch, shucking open my ribs
until they filled like kites and rode the simple coils of air:

your hands, teaching me breath.

Night Pines

Cresting into an oceanic night, dunes root
in razor grass and shroud the coastal lights
sitting somewhere behind, picked off against
the blue-black and bruising sky.
This horizon

is the balance, point and counter
for vanishing. Birds swirl there like sucked ships,
and the sea unrolls from it in lazy folds
shaken out towards the pebble beach,
lying low and curved, its stones dumb, felled.

There's a stretch behind the trees that takes off right,
the trail shallow and young, shadows holding green
behind your closed lids. Here, the path forms
a far-off river bend, and the white sand echoes
the stark twist and shine of you in pines.

Holkham

The house hangs heavy by water
as if awaiting the courage
to fill the last pocket with gravel
and stumble forward and down.

Deer line the drive
with an oaky, fearful musk
raising a mewling low and deep,
rising skittish as a shower.

The small lights of the town are waking.
From the hilltop we stop to fill our faces with sunrise,
and again at the cattle grid we pause:
breathing through the air we won't cross.

At this time, the grasses sit dewy as eyes.
An impatience drapes sun between land and sky
and illiterate trees read the sway of salted wind
following at our backs from the sea.

Our legs churn through the spaces
we always leave between
the thought and the hurt –
a silence sharp and base as turning fruit.

Gillying

In this gull-lipped boat
we cast off, second skinned
by a scummy low tide,
low hipped in silt.

We fight the current to hover
over a sunken salt marsh,
where we take up rods, arm
small buckets, gilly for crabs.

Taut at my wrists, the string
twists with rotted fat, baptised
in the Norfolk tide, raised up in
waving pincers. A last supper.

Nothing like fresh meat, leaching
sea and broiled in its own salt,
a plain of sand our tablecloth
our fingers forking each morsel;

the suck and swell of our mouths,
the undertow of impatience
elemental in our bodies on that
beach. The night seeps in.

Somewhere beyond Holkham bay,
wavelets scuttle, raised on their
haunches and whipped up
by the moon, that ultimate pull

of the half-familiar. In the dark it is clean
malice. The tug of the ocean compassing
the earth matching your finger,
pinholing my pulse.

Gillying (v): To fish for crabs; to caress

34

Altitude

Like walking a wire, my feet follow
carefully, and behind my left eye is
an ache I mistake for missing you.

One inch wrong leaves me reeling.
My ankle rolls and I lift off,
find myself wingless.

Banff

for Sue Goyette

Morning after snow.
The wind tidal, stacking
into our open room.

Below, the gentle bowl of town
sits sifted through white, bricks
hazelnut against cream.

Your breathing back is turned
and dreaming, and I am left waking
to reckon with silence.

Tor

We came here to give praise for this moor.
The slow, turning fog of it,
the silvered shunt of its wind-clad rain,
the clodded grass and stealth of rabbit holes
pitted against our ankles as we sink up
its planted, routed depths.

Up top we level out against the air,
bevelled against the tor's slick surface,
and I feel merely cherished, cupped
into the weather,
as though we –
he and me –

are the last pieces left to tether
the earth's shattered continents back together.

Whitstable Natives

Forget the violence,
of blade versus shell and the blood
I sucked from your fingers.

You are bringing me the ocean
on a plate, shrouded and steaming with ice;
oyster-bedded. Now feel

the shuck of your tongue as it
swallows down the sweet-fleshed pearl.
Listen: you can taste the sea.

Pebble

It sat beside them on the dinner table
pressing down a page as he read

to her, against the wind
from the sea marshes,

dropping gull-cries like song
through the open window,

and later stretched the red distance
between his palm and her nape,

called down a week of rain,
some darkness, a stitch of time.

The night sinks into its element –
a simple grace of silence –

as the pebble on the mantel
unhatches the sea.

Pulse

after Elizabeth Philips

This room was once
another colour –
it phases between white
and all the other shades
of light falling in
from the passing day.

I watch for change,
but never catch the shift,
follow instead
the cut and shimmer
of your back cooling
into sleep and think

you were once
another person –
with other kinds
of touch, a different
way of folding
into someone else.

I may have stayed steady under
each body I've lain by, though
never more mortal
nor more known, than under
the pulse and stretch of you.

A Perfect Gift

I could bring you three
songbirds for your birthday

have them sing out,
lemon-throated, or

sling hook
an indian summer

shot through with
starlight-heavy nights

or unhaul from my chest
that precise mechanism

for knowing you.
I could make us

strangers again,
just to relearn you.

wide-shining

Tiberius
for John

I was sent from the earth a king and came back a fish.
I grew from grit and salt, blind as a pearl, my gills tainted with bile
I gleaned from anemones, and azure slugs bound to rock.
Through pure will I grew teeth from my mouth and from my belly,
teeth that I dragged across the ocean bed to spear crabs clean through.
When I fed, I fed well, on the soft hearts of snails eked
from their shells and on the sweetmeats of urchins.
I raised myself beautiful, captured greens from the prisms of water
and purples from the poison of snakes, sucked them clean
through my cheeks to stain my scales rainbow.

I was a prize, of course, miracle-mimicking-god,
so I offered death, ripping fishbone twine and snapping men's fingers,
guiding boats through triangle currents that pulled only ever down.
Someone started a rumour that I needed silver hooks –
got one through my lip once, liked the look –
but in the end it was a girl's red silk that drew me in, trout-like,
when it caressed my serrated belly as she swilled it at the shore.
Her hands were thin, spliced wires, shocking at my throat.
She ran with me, until we were gasping both
as she poured me to the feet of her father.

I burned my insides bitter, churned at their legs in hellish arcs
But he wrapped his wrists in leather and lifted my bulk to the sun,
rubbed seawater into my flesh and carried me through pathless rocks
to a king, to be his honour, a salty offering, rare.

What happened between was beyond my sight,
but soon I was in crueller hands and the man was
on the ground trussed as a sow, squealing mercy, and I,
the mimicry-blessing, was salved to his skin,
rubbed 'til we bled each other out,
and lay milk-eyed on marble,
slabbed, as I was always wont to be.

When I come back,
I will come back as sickness,
sit nubbed into a sane man's brain,
and slowly rot him insane.

Pandora

My back to the room / I hear them buzz / let my hands / lift and drop
and they pour / their million wings / beating into the world
fear cruelty avarice / all the many names / for pain
and I have made man / complete and entire
with the simple / hinge of a lid
at my fingertip.

Echo

In between your visits, I live in this tree,
taking in the whole wide stretch & weight of the sky.
When you begin your morning walk, in botched copy I follow –
we cross the obsolete stream, where narcissi hang their bell-heads,
bending in long dissent towards the shallows.
You break them at the stem & we set off between the narrows,
me dancing your steps off the shadows in perfect half rhyme.
Here you whistle, and I join in, a quarter-beat behind your beat.
I throw you, so you try to shrug me off like a heavy-shouldered coat,
but I cross-stitch behind you, trailing like a loyal dog. Hounding.
I do enjoy these jaunts, & miss you when you leave the kiln
of our forest for your open field-walk home,
your five-year-empty house.

I hope it won't be long till your return, till next
you carry me like prayer beads in your pocket,
& go through the wood whistling,
& like little starlings, I fly your music back.

Starver

Daisy did not eat to-
day.
More for us.

Daisy did not eat this next day.
Nor this one
even though to-day we had lamb.

It's been a week.
Two hard-boiled eggs left on her desk
stink out the house.

Mam frets. Da shouts.

Daisy watches the hills from our window
and will not speak to me
even when I ask what she sees.

I sit beside her and watch the shadow grow
and swallow our house.
Daisy's eyes are shadows swallowing, too.

Mam beats her with a wooden spoon
across the face.
Smack! Smack! Smack!

Her cheekbone swells
and her stomach does too,
though it can only be full of air.

A month gone.
Daisy lies, the rack of her body
stretched out.

Da charges 3 for a peek
5 for a touch, and I watch her with
Mam's wooden spoon

in case someone gets too close.
Priest says she's living on Holy Spirit.
I know she's rotting.

To-night Daisy spoke,
and asked me to take her to our window
and we talked a little.

I think to-night's the final night.

I let her kiss my cheek
though she reeks stale water
and I told her that I loved her, too.

Next day,
when Mam asks God why?
holding what's left of Daisy

I say
I think she saw sickness in the hills
and got out while she still had time.

Kitsunetsuki

The borrowing starts at birth.

Her first cry snaps across her mother's ear
like a slap. The village wakes
and prays. The stars strike out.

Next, cradle cap that seethes with ticks,
and in certain lights, her scalp burns auburn,
her skin furs, her mouth muzzles, her lobes twitch.

It brings her new language – cry and screech –
strings her along the streets in search of scraps,
wets her mouth on sight of rats.

At fifteen she leaves for the trees,
burrows beneath corpse mushrooms
and suckles at her wrist for a taste of home.

Her spine curves, and her shoulders firm
to better bear the four-quarter lurch,
the stark absurdity of her form.

It leaves her sudden as a shower
in her eighteenth year, cracks out
through her ribs, crests her breasts.

They find her bent beneath blossom
wound-and-mouth-agape, trailing blood,
claw roots empty on her knuckles,

fox-tang stalking the ground.

Medusa

Days when I needed to slough my skin
stitch the wounds with fish bone twine
so I could suffer as I meant to; my statement
of intent. Days filled with stone, spent with only me,
days spent alone. Days I was a dissenter of my own

cause, days when I'd think to drop glasses
and shuffle across the floor on my hands and knees
just to bleed. Days spent watching the unravelling
and catching the threads just in time, stuffing the
secret into my head, fistfuls of hissing, black-eyed scales.

Days when I forgot. Days when I could not.
Days when days turned faster than a cricket
chirruping their victory on green legs that
I pulled off, clawed off until I caught the sun
and stared until my eyes were scarred with
daytime stars. Most days though, follow on.
It's a case of taking them, one by one.

Hermaphroditus

for Iain Banks

She takes me up
hard and
    worries my skin
drags nails across my chest
in imitation love

she practises
    cruelty with each stroke
and shouts for our union
our never-parting

parts me from myself
with her wish

splits me monstrous,
    halves me entire,
    smoothes out
    that last
        skitter
    of flesh

my nerves buzz
    as her body
burns into mine.

Rhea's Revenge

You have made a litany of our lives,
husband, worthy of any myth. How
did they taste, I wonder? Each
small boy slipped down your gullet.
I trembled beneath your body as you sweated
out their sweetness, sweated in the next.

Take in enough water
to layer your pain,
you'll need it on your lungs
to stop the sounds.
Imagine each son
weighting your gut.

When I finally release, I'll haul you home
to prop against the hearth,
still wet from the sea. I'll cook samphire
in tight shoals of butter and lime,
and offer it to your conched mouth, massage
'til swallowed and watch your belly swell.

Later,
I'll cut you
groin to teeth
bury our children's bones,
the one black stone,
then feast.

Leda

Then the light opened and closed about her;
slumped angels onto the carpet,
trumpeting grotesquely, their shadows
angled into corners, into anywhere and
anything but that safe, squared certainty.
Then music grew monstrous;
grew larger and filled the air,
feathered and full-bellied,
web-toed as a demon and hot,
but white. Pure white. And soft.
Then the gilding nudges at her lap
a forgotten currency of head and tail
coins forged in the heat of lightening
and thunderclaps, her heart slaps in her chest,
throws up muddying blood to her head.
Then wings, leaving the darkness
no space, no place not to look
to be sure not to see as they pin her
in her chair and the last of the glare swells up
rears into the serpent neck that snips at her throat.
Then she is absented from herself,
poured, rolled, molten, gold as the light at her feet,
shot through with hardening gems, mined roughly
as a coalface, as wholly,
until her thighs chaff with myth.

It leaves her opened, gift-like, on the stairwell
her lips bruised, her eyelids split as fruit,
wrists snapped back in greeting or farewell
as seeds aping love take root.

Danae

Your arrival?

Heraldic, triumphal, callous and cruel – you slap me onto all fours – I see you've done this before.

You form-shift as is your gift; swan, bat, bull (I shudder at that), a lily-flower, smoked ice and, finally, how nice, a golden shower. My jaw is a rictus, my legs skew under you and I know it is hopeless. Try to enjoy it you said, and I play dead. Slot box, slatted, mouse and cat, unhinged at the rim of me, pelted, melded, bone-tired and blood-sore, and still there is more.

Outside my father kneels at your stone feet and prays for you to bless him. Your coining eyes turn away. You pluck yourself out of me, fast and loose-changing into light. My eyes clenched tight, I am left beast-panting and baby-fat, and call for my family. They tell me I was fated by the act that damns me. No more, Jove. Now, will you be sated?

Circe

Daily I watch my men.

Their suffering is
carefully curated –
a pinkening for each time
they denied me,

a trotter for each time
they forced me,
and finally –
that tassel of a tail.

I end the day with a meal,
(predictably porcine),
after an hour scrubbing
shit from under my nails.

I'd go mad,
but I cannot forget my name,
a dying fall
fat in their mouths.

Persephone

Most mornings I can barely stand to look at this
something-like-happiness misting our periphery,
an epiphany spat out like pips from our tongues,
all our half-sung songs stringing along behind us,
and you, dark god, perfect weight above me, telling
me you love me and me drop dropping droplets through
your hand my stolid body turning liquid as sand and running
our fierce current fast as silver-quick fish, my flick-flecking lips
biting like teeth as I shoal beneath you, held so tight I can barely breathe.

The shift of the seasons sinks us,
and at my brink I tip through
summer autumn winter spring
– all the fast-spin of cold and heat –
fells me as I fall back replete,
my heart beating pomegranate red,
jawing my mouthful of seeds.

Selkie

On the emptied beach I turn from the waves,
from the smooth tug of the Yesnaby tide
towards you, backed by limestone caves,
then unstitch myself at the hip and step out.

I have come for you. Open your hands to me
in the rain, in the dark cloister of Skaill bay.
Listen: how the sea shrugs itself up the beach
struggles to cast itself off, like a shadow at midday.

After, I grope for my pelt in the sand.
It is quiet now, the sea far out and closed,
a riddle I forgot I was meant to know.
A tithe of scum wrinkles my toes.

You sing me lullabies, wrap me in your history
until it feels almost-shared. You kiss me
until you're dizzy with sea-breath, and fling
your laugh out to the heaving black.

A whole night passes, then is gone.
The day drags the water back up to us
and I drape myself into form.
At the tide line I pause, turn again to you.

Let me
drop my skin. I never liked the sea.
Let me
lie down with you again.
Let me
stay. I could love you.

The Minotaur's Mother

Afterwards, they ask me if I knew
and when

and how did I feel about it?
And I say no

but, really, when was it? Because
yes, I knew and

yes, I always loved you.

Was it when I woke torn and bleeding
from the bull?

Or when I felt the kick in my abdomen
signalling life?

Or when I felt you churning my insides
like cud?

Or shook with the strength of your heartbeat
at night?

Or was it only when I sensed you ready to come
into the world

and called for the midwife to bring blankets
as I felt

the burr of horn caught in the hinge
of my pelvis

then the soft split as you eased yourself through
and I spilled you

into the waiting room, into a deep and
terrible silence?

Acknowledgments

Some of these poems have appeared previously in *Agenda, Broadsheets, The Cadaverine, Cake Poetry, Catweazle Magazine, Coffee House Poetry, the delinquent, Ink, Sweat and Tears, Inky Needles, The Lamp, Magma, Other Poetry, The Poor Press* and in the anthologies *Appletree Writers' In On The Tide 2013* and *Sentinel Annual Literary Anthology 2012*.

'Grace' won the Yeovil Literary Prize for Poetry 2013.

Poems in the section titled 'wide-shining' are taken from a collection of the same name, published in June 2013 by 79 rat press. My thanks to editor Dan Holloway for allowing a selection to be reproduced here.

Particular thanks are due to the Gatehouse team, Tom Corbett, John Burnside, Patricia McCarthy, Sue Goyette, Tom de Freston, Daisy Johnson, Sarvat Hasin, Agnes Davis, Jo Hemmant, and my creative writing cohorts in Oxford and Banff for their detailed feedback and encouragement.

I am very grateful to the Expansionists Project and the Banff Centre for residencies and writing time.

As ever, my deepest gratitude to my family for their unstinting love and support.

Finally, thanks to Tom. For everything.